1ST
IN FASHION

LOUIS RÉARD
BIKINI DESIGNER

REBECCA FELIX

Checkerboard
Library

An Imprint of Abdo Publishing
abdopublishing.com

ABDOPUBLISHING.COM

Published by Abdo Publishing, a division of ABDO, PO Box 398166, Minneapolis, Minnesota 55439. Copyright © 2018 by Abdo Consulting Group, Inc. International copyrights reserved in all countries. No part of this book may be reproduced in any form without written permission from the publisher. Checkerboard Library™ is a trademark and logo of Abdo Publishing.

Printed in the United States of America, North Mankato, Minnesota
062017
092017

THIS BOOK CONTAINS
RECYCLED MATERIALS

Design: Emily O'Malley, Mighty Media, Inc.
Production: Emily O'Malley, Mighty Media, Inc.
Series Editor: Katherine Hengel Frankowski
Cover Photographs: Getty Images (left); Shutterstock (right)
Interior Photographs: Alamy, pp. 15, 23; AP Images, p. 21; Getty Images, pp. 13, 17; iStockphoto, pp. 25 (middle), 27; Shutterstock, pp. 5, 10, 19, 25 (top), 25 (bottom); Wikimedia Commons, pp. 7, 9, 24 (top), 24 (middle), 24 (bottom)

Publisher's Cataloging-in-Publication Data

Names: Felix, Rebecca, author.
Title: Louis Réard: bikini designer / by Rebecca Felix.
Other titles: Bikini designer
Description: Minneapolis, MN : Abdo Publishing, 2018. | Series: First in fashion |
    Includes bibliographical references and index.
Identifiers: LCCN 2016962504 | ISBN 9781532110764 (lib. bdg.) |
    ISBN 9781680788617 (ebook)
Subjects: LCSH: Réard, Louis, 1897-1984--Juvenile literature. | Fashion designer--
    France--Biography--Juvenile literature.
Classification: DDC 746.9 [B]--dc23
LC record available at http://lccn.loc.gov/2016962504

CONTENTS

SHOCKING SWIMWEAR

〰〰〰

It's a hot summer day. You are headed to a busy beach to cool off. You arrive and see some kids building sand castles. Others are swimming. One group is playing a game of beach volleyball.

Most of the boys and men are wearing swim trunks. And many of the girls and women are wearing two-piece suits. These two-piece suits come in many different styles. They allow girls to swim, play, and move freely. Today, these two-piece suits are called bikinis.

Louis Réard (REE-eerd) designed and named the first bikini. Réard's creation was not the first two-piece swimsuit. But it was the smallest the world had ever seen! Before Réard's bikinis, swimwear was much more modest. Réard's design shocked the world, but it soon became a fashion icon. For the last 70 years, bikinis have been popular on beaches around the world.

Bikinis are still one of the most popular swimsuit styles for women and girls. People wear bikinis in many colors and prints.

AUTOMOBILE ENGINEER

Louis Réard was born in 1897. Much of his life is unknown to historians, including his birthplace. Some reports say Réard was born in France. Others say he was born in Switzerland. Conflicting claims about Réard's life are common.

It is believed that Réard lived near Paris, France, for most of his life. As an adult, he became an automobile engineer. In the 1930s, he worked for French automobile manufacturer Renault. There, Réard created many cars.

In the 1940s, Réard left the automobile industry and joined the fashion world. His mother owned a company in Paris that made **lingerie**. Réard took over her company and began designing clothing instead of cars.

In his new line of work, Réard designed a two-piece swimsuit. It was unlike anything beachgoers at the time had ever seen. But the garment had its roots in ancient athletic wear.

Réard worked on many car models at Renault. These included the Primaquatre (*shown*) and the Nervasport.

SWIMSUITS OF THE PAST

Two-piece garments date back to 1400 BCE. Ancient Greek **urns** show women wearing the garments while playing sports. It is believed this style of clothing helped women move their arms and legs freely. They could run, jump, catch, and kick.

Similar two-piece garments were worn for thousands of years. In fact, they appear in Roman artwork from the 1300s CE. But in the centuries that followed, society's feelings about women's garments changed. This was especially true with swimwear.

In the 1800s, many **cultures** believed women should not be seen swimming. During those times, women who wanted to swim were carried into the water on horse-drawn carriages. Once the carriage was deep enough in the water, women could jump out and swim.

Women in two-piece garments are featured in ancient Greek artwork. The women's tops are bandeaus. Their bottoms are similar to loincloths.

The swimsuits these women wore made swimming difficult. The garments were made of wool or **flannel** and covered the entire body. These fabrics were used because they did not become transparent when wet. But they became very heavy. Female swimmers had to hold onto ropes attached to shore to stay afloat.

9

MODESTY IS A MUST

Modesty was in style worldwide into the 1900s. Both men and women could get in trouble for showing too

Before the invention of the bikini, it was considered improper to show one's navel. Navels weren't allowed to be shown on TV or in movies!

much skin. In 1907, an Australian woman visiting a US beach was arrested. She was wearing a formfitting bathing suit that showed her legs.

Over the next few decades, modest styles stayed in fashion on and off the beach. However, in the 1930s, some celebrities started showing more skin. They wore dresses and tops that revealed their stomachs.

US fashion designer Claire McCardell applied this trend to women's swimwear. She created a one-piece suit with side cutouts. Soon, two-piece bathing suits were being worn too. These suits had long tops that covered most of the wearer's stomach. The bottoms rose above the **navel**.

These 1930s suits were still considered fairly modest. However, they were a step toward smaller, more revealing swimwear. Such styles would become common in the coming decades.

NAME CHANGES

For centuries, swimming garments were referred to as bathing suits. Then, in the 1920s, swimwear company Jantzen began calling the garments swimming suits. It was thought that this name sounded sportier. The name stuck! Today, it is often shortened to swimsuits.

WAR RATIONS

In the 1940s, much of the world took part in **World War II**. Many countries **rationed** their goods. All available materials had to be used for the war effort. Fabric was needed for soldiers' clothing, not swimsuits. Having fewer resources was limiting for many business owners. But for Réard, it sparked an idea.

He had seen French women rolling up the edges of their swimsuits. They did this to expose more skin to the sun. The more skin they showed, the more skin they could tan! Réard realized that these women would appreciate a smaller bathing suit.

THE RISE OF SUN TANNING

For many years, tan skin was not considered fashionable in Europe and the United States. But in the 1920s, fashion designer Coco Chanel went on a beach vacation. She got very tan from being in the sun and was photographed. Soon, other women were tanning to imitate her!

Réard is most famous for the bikini, but he also designed other beachwear and women's clothing.

With **rationing** in effect, Réard already had a material shortage. So instead of making fewer items, he'd just use less fabric. But French designer Jacques Heim had a similar idea. So Réard and Heim began a race. Who could bring small swimsuits to the world first?

SKY WARS

In the autumn of 1945, **World War II** ended. The public's mood became more **lighthearted**. This shift created the perfect **environment** to release a new kind of swimsuit. Heim and Réard hurried to complete their creations.

Both men worked hard to quickly produce their small swimsuits. In May 1946, it seemed Heim was closer. He even began advertising on **Mediterranean** beaches. Heim hired a pilot to fly over the beaches with a banner. The banner said that Heim had made "the world's smallest bathing suit."

Réard heard about Heim's airborne ad. He was not sure how small Heim's suit would be. But he decided to make sure his would be even tinier. He also decided he'd hire a plane to advertise his product too.

FASHION FACTOID

Heim called his swimsuit the Atome. *Atome* is French for "atom," which is the smallest particle that exists.

Jacques Heim was an accomplished designer of women's clothing and costumes for theater and movies.

Réard's ad flew over beachgoers in the **French Riviera** three weeks after Heim's ad did. Like Heim's plane, Réard's pulled a banner. It said, "smaller than the smallest bathing suit in the world."

THE BIG REVEAL

In June 1946, Heim released his two-piece swimsuit. It was indeed small, especially its top. The bottoms were still quite modest though. They rose high enough to cover the wearer's **navel**.

Réard released his two-piece suit one month later. Like Heim's suit, Réard's featured a small **bandeau** top. But the bottoms on Réard's suit were much, much smaller. They were made from two triangles. String ties held the two triangles together. It was the first swimsuit to show the wearer's navel.

Réard called his swimsuit a bikini, after the Bikini Atoll. This is a chain of islands in the South Pacific Ocean. The islands were **controversial** because the United States used them to test nuclear bombs. Réard hoped naming his swimsuit after the islands would also cause a stir.

On July 5, 1946, the world first saw Réard's bikini on Micheline Bernardini. She was a well-known French dancer. Bernardini wore Réard's bikini at a famous public pool in Paris. Réard knew the press would be there. So, he designed the bikini's fabric to look like newsprint.

Réard was right! His bikini was big news. It got the attention of both the press and the public. Réard received more than 50,000 pieces of fan mail. However, not everyone was impressed with Réard's creation.

Réard at work in his studio in the 1950s

BIKINI MARKETING & BANS

The **debut** of Réard's teeny bikinis caused a major splash. He had not only created the world's smallest swimsuits. He had a talent for **marketing** them too. Réard packaged each bikini in a matchbox. This proved to shoppers just how small the suits were!

Selling bikinis in matchboxes wasn't Réard's only marketing trick. He developed a catchy **demonstration** too. He'd tell people there was "one way" to identify a true bikini. Then he'd pull an entire bikini through a wedding ring.

Réard was great at publicizing the bikini's small size. But were people ready for such small, **skimpy** swimsuits?

FASHION FACTOID

At first, many models refused to wear Réard's bikini. They felt it was too small and revealing. Each suit was made from just 30 square inches (194 sq cm) of fabric.

Many Americans resisted the bikini at first. But the swimsuit was embraced in the French Riviera, a tourist destination for celebrities and wealthy people.

Many people around the world thought bikinis were **scandalous**. They felt the swimsuit drew too much attention to females' bodies. These people believed wearing a bikini was shameful.

Many world leaders agreed. Some were upset enough to take legal action. Government officials in Italy made bikinis illegal to wear in public. Belgium, Spain, and Australia did too. Most US citizens also believed bikinis were overly **risqué**. US bikini sales began in 1947, but they were very slow.

STAR SUPPORT

Despite the bans, some women still wanted to wear bikinis. In fact, for some women, the bans added to the bikini's appeal. Beginning in the 1940s, many women felt a rising sense of **empowerment**. Women were entering the workforce and gaining independence. These women did not want to be told what to wear. They welcomed the chance to **defy** the bikini bans.

The 1950s would be a turning point for bikinis worldwide. This had everything to do with Brigitte Bardot. Bardot was a famous French actor. In 1952, she starred in *The Girl in the Bikini*. It was one of the first films to feature a bikini.

To promote the film, Bardot visited famous beaches wearing her bikini. Many photos of her in the small suit were published. And, the film was shown in theaters worldwide. This helped bikinis become more acceptable.

Brigitte Bardot wore a bikini on the beach during the 1953 Cannes Film Festival. It immediately drew more attention to both the bikini and French cinema.

Thanks to Bardot, bikini sales started to slowly rise in many nations. This would not be the bikini's only sales boost from the film world. In the 1960s, the real boost would come from a new type of US film.

BEACH PARTY BIKINIS

Teenagers worldwide have often valued freedom and independence. In the 1960s, US filmmakers released beach party films reflecting these values. The films featured US teens hanging out on beaches. The teens in these films did what they wanted away from adults. Swimsuits, including bikinis, were their main costumes.

Beach party films were wildly popular, especially with teens. The more American filmgoers saw bikinis, the less shocking they became. Americans began to view bikinis as less alarming. Soon, bikinis were a common sight on US beaches.

By the 1960s, Réard was not the only one making teeny two-pieces. Once bikinis became popular,

FASHION FACTOID

Pop singer Brian Hyland wrote a song about bikinis in the 1960s. "Itsy Bitsy Teeny Weenie Yellow Polkadot Bikini" is still famous today.

STARRING
BOB
CUMMINGS
DOROTHY
MALONE
FRANKIE
AVALON
ANNETTE
FUNICELLO
HARVEY
LEMBECK
JODY
McCREA
JOHN
ASHLEY
ALSO STARRING
MOREY
AMSTERDAM
AND SIX
EVA

AMERICAN INTERNATIONAL'S

It's what happens when **10,000** kids meet on **5,000** Beach Blankets!

Beach Party was the first of seven popular films starring Annette Funicello and Frankie Avalon.

competitors began selling their own versions. However, Réard had **trademarked** the word *bikini*. So, none of his competitors could use the term.

Despite Réard's trademark, *bikini* eventually became a **generic** term. It's now used to refer to any small, two-piece suit. *Bikini* has become a classic fashion description. It is still widely used today.

FASHION
TIME MACHINE

BATHING GOWN, 1700s–1800s In the 1700s and 1800s, women wore ankle-length dresses with long sleeves, called bathing gowns, to the beach. Bathing gowns were very heavy and made swimming difficult.

MAILLOT, 1910s The first maillots were sleeveless and ended in high-cut shorts. They allowed more freedom of movement than most previous swimsuits. Today, the maillot is called a one-piece.

TWO-PIECE AND BIKINI, 1930s–1950s As sunbathing became a popular activity, swimsuits got smaller and smaller. The bikini was invented as a result! It remains the most popular swimsuit style.

COMPETITION SWIMSUIT, 1970s In the 1970s, elastane was added to one-piece swimsuits for Olympic athletes. This created a stretchy fabric, known as spandex. It fit tightly to the athlete's body, cutting down on resistance and increasing speed.

TANKINI, 1990s The tankini is a two-piece swimsuit that covers the **midriff**. It was invented in 1998 by swimsuit designer Anne Cole. The tankini provides an option in between a bikini and a one-piece. Nearly one-third of swimsuits sold today are tankinis!

BURKINI, 2000s The burkini covers the entire body except for the face, hands, and feet. It was designed for people who follow religious traditions of modesty. But it is also worn by those who choose to cover their skin for personal or medical reasons.

SWIMWEAR STAPLE

The bikini's popularity kept rising, though Réard faded out of the spotlight. Very little is known about his life after the 1940s. It is believed he owned a swimsuit shop in Paris, and he continued to sell bikinis there.

In his later years, Réard was interviewed about designing the bikini. He was surprised that people were interested in his story. He seemed content to live a private life. In 1980, he and his wife, Michelle, moved to Lausanne, Switzerland. Réard died there four years later, in 1984, at the age of 87.

Today, bikinis are worn at beaches and pools worldwide. Female film and television actors often wear them while filming. Models wear bikinis during photoshoots and on fashion runways.

FASHION FACTOID

In 2011, a solar-powered bikini was invented. It can charge an electronic device using the sun's energy!

Beach volleyball players often wear bikinis while competing. From 1996 to 2012, the bikini was the required uniform for female Olympic volleyball players.

Modern bikinis come in in many materials and colors. They can be sporty, sparkly, modest, or **risqué**. Many bikinis are even smaller than Réard's original design!

Réard set out to create something that would shock the world. His **scandalous** swimsuit certainly did. It also became a classic piece of swimwear. The bikini made a splash and changed fashion forever.

TIMELINE

X X X   X X X

1897

Louis Réard is born.

1940s

Réard quits his job as an automobile engineer to take over his mother's lingerie business.

1946

On July 5, Réard reveals his bikini at a pool in Paris, France.

1947

Bikinis are sold in the United States.

1952

Actor Brigitte Bardot wears a bikini in *The Girl in the Bikini*. The bikini's popularity rises worldwide.

1960s

Bikinis are featured in beach party films. The swimsuit catches on in the United States.

1984

Réard dies in Switzerland on September 16 at the age of 87.

1998

The tankini is invented.

GLOSSARY

bandeau—a band-like covering for a woman's chest.

controversial—of or relating to a discussion marked by strongly different views.

culture—the customs, arts, and tools of a nation or a people at a certain time.

debut—a first appearance.

defy—to challenge or refuse to follow.

demonstration—the act of showing or explaining something by using examples.

empowerment—a social process that helps people gain control over their own lives.

environment—the conditions or circumstances surrounding something.

flannel—a soft fabric made of cotton or wool.

French Riviera—the Mediterranean coast of southeast France.

generic—not having a brand name.

lighthearted—without cares or worries.

lingerie—women's nightclothes or undergarments.

marketing—the process of advertising or promoting an item for sale.

Mediterranean—relating to the Mediterranean Sea or to the lands or peoples around it.

midriff—the middle area of the human body.

navel—the belly button.

ration—to control the amount of something people can have.

risqué—almost indecent.

scandalous—harmful to one's reputation.

skimpy—revealing.

trademark—something such as a word that identifies a certain company. Something trademarked cannot be used by others without permission.

urn—a container that is often shaped like a vase and has a closed top. Urns are often used to hold the ashes of someone who has been cremated.

World War II—from 1939 to 1945, fought in Europe, Asia, and Africa. Great Britain, France, the United States, the Soviet Union, and their allies were on one side. Germany, Italy, Japan, and their allies were on the other side.

WEBSITES

To learn more about First in Fashion, visit **abdobooklinks.com**. These links are routinely monitored and updated to provide the most current information available.

INDEX